KU-198-484

Care of Clothes

JANE ASHELFORD

The National Trust

First published in 1997 by National Trust (Enterprises) Ltd
36 Queen Anne's Gate, London SW1H 9AS

Text © Jane Ashelford 1997
Advice on care of clothes © Shelley Tobin 1997
Registered Charity No. 205846
ISBN 0 7078 0223 7

A catalogue record for this book is available from the British Library

Apart from fair dealing for the purposes of research or private study, or criticism or review, as permitted under the Copyright, Designs and Patents Act, 1988, this publication may only be reproduced, stored or transmitted, in any form or by any means, with the prior permission in writing of the publishers, or in the case of reprographic reproduction in accordance with the terms of the licences issued by the Copyright Licensing Agency.

Picture research by Sophie Blair and Margaret Willes

Designed by Peter Guy

Production by Bob Towell

Printed and bound in Hong Kong
Mandarin Offset Limited

Front cover: *Detail of the Dry Laundry at Castle Ward, Co. Down*
Frontispiece: *A crimping iron at Castle Ward*
Back cover: *A storage case for dressing-table items dating from the 1660s. The embroidered brocade case contained a flat mirror backed with the same material and a brush.*

Introduction

It is difficult today to realise how much effort was devoted to the laundering of clothes in the past – technology has released us from the onerous and labour-intensive task of washing and drying. Crease-free fabrics can be bundled into a washing-machine programmed to deal with every man-made and natural fibre, and electric irons smooth out the remaining wrinkles with their precision steam jets. The labour-saving devices described here will consequently appear antiquated, but to a housewife of the sixteenth, seventeenth or eighteenth centuries they would have seemed nothing short of miraculous.

Most of the text for this little book was originally written for a very large book – *The Art of Dress: Clothes and Society 1500–1914* published by the National Trust in 1996. In it, Jane Ashelford explores the social aspects of dress: how styles were conveyed; where materials and clothes were purchased; what all levels of society wore – from duke to serving boy; and all ages – from swaddling bands to widow's weeds. Since the book was published we have been plied with questions on how our ancestors looked after their clothes – from how they were cleaned using wood ash and urine, to how and where the bulky clothing of the past was stored in the days before that twentieth-century innovation – the coat-hanger.

We also found that many of our questioners had old clothes handed down to them, and wanted advice on how to keep them in good condition. For that reason we have included hints on how best to preserve your clothes for future generations, written by Shelley Tobin, curator of one of the National Trust's costume collections at Killerton House in Devon. Shelley looks after over eight thousand items of costume spanning four hundred years, from a 1690s gentleman's waistcoat to a series of 1920s cocktail dresses. Each year she presents an exhibition featuring a small number of these items: the theme for autumn 1996 was, by coincidence, on the care of clothes.

Margaret Willes, Publisher

U NTIL the seventeenth century, the most basic way of washing clothes was to beat them clean in a stream or a communal wash-house. However, to remove greasy dirt such as tallow and fat, clothes were first soaked in an alkaline solution known as lye, which was prepared two or three days before the wash began. Fine white ashes were collected from furnaces and ovens and placed in a wooden sieve over a tub. Water was poured through and stirred so that it became impregnated with the alkaline salts released from the ashes. In areas where wood ash was not available, the reddish-grey ashes of burnt bracken were used instead. The greasy or stained laundry would be placed in a wooden tub called a 'buck', the lye was poured over it and left for a few hours. The tub was then drained by a small tap at the base and the process repeated until the lye came through clean – which meant the clothes were ready to be rinsed and dried.

It was a lengthy business. In January 1660, Elizabeth Pepys would have woken the maids at four in the morning to begin the wash, and Pepys describes how he sat up 'till the bell-man came by and cried "Past one of the clock and a cold, frosty, windy morning". Then I went to bed and left my wife and maid a-washing still.'

For those who could afford it, whitsters (those who whiten things) would do the 'buck wash' for housewives who did not want to wash and dry their clothes at home. In *The Merry Wives of Windsor* Shakespeare used the 'buck wash' as a comic device. Falstaff was unceremoniously bundled into the buck basket 'rammed in with foul shirts and smocks, socks, foul stockings, greasy napkins', and then carried to Datchet Mead, a meadow between Windsor and the River Thames where he was emptied into 'the muddy ditch close by the Thames side'.

Detail of laundrywomen from a nineteenth-century print attributed to A. de Fios, now at The Vyne, Hampshire.

O P E N spaces around London were very much the domain of whitsters in the sixteenth and seventeenth centuries. On 12 August 1667, Samuel Pepys recorded in his diary that, 'My wife and maids [are] gone over the water to Whitster's with their clothes, this being the first time of her trying this way of washing her linen.' Elizabeth Pepys caught a ferry at Whitehall Steps and crossed to either Lambeth Marsh or Southwark. When they did not return until the evening of the following day at 'nine at night, a dark rainy night' Pepys became concerned but, undaunted, Elizabeth repeated the process the following year – and her husband found he had 'little company at home'.

London housewives also took their washing to Moorfields, just to the north of the City, where there were rows of hooked posts. Wet washing was attached to the hooks, then wound round tightly until the water had been squeezed out. It would be laid out to dry on the ground or hung on a series of clothes lines. An early sixteenth-century writer compared the 'acres of old linen' spread out on the ground to 'the fields of Cartagena when the five months shift of the whole fleet are washed and spread'.

Laundry in country houses was dealt with in a similar way. Walled drying greens were constructed close to the laundry offices and are still *in situ* at Castle Ward in County Down, Calke Abbey in Derbyshire and Dunham Massey in Cheshire. Clothes would be delicately scented if they were dried draped over rosemary and lavender hedges, but a careful eye had to be kept out for thieves. Autolycus, the 'snapper-up of unconsidered trifles' in *The Winter's Tale* enjoys the spring because it brings out 'The white sheet bleaching on the hedge.'

Detail from the Copperplate Map, now in the Museum of London, drawn in 1575. It shows the area around Shoreditch, just to the north east of the City, with Moorfields where housewives took their laundry to lay out and dry.

SHORDICH

S. M. Spittl

Busshoppes gate Strete

Fynnesb Courte.

Blak hows.

Dogg hows.

Bedlame

MOOR FIELD.

Giardin di Pietro

Bedlam Gate

S. Bwich

MOOR GATE.

All holyes ni the Wall

BVSSHOPPES GATE.

PAPYE

SOAP was also used for laundry, but it was much more expensive than lye. It was made by boiling lye with animal fat, a commodity much in demand for other household uses, such as cooking and the manufacture of candles. Salt and perfume were added to the mixture, and the soft compound was then formed into small balls. The accounts of the Shuttleworth family of Gawthorpe Hall in Lancashire mention both lye and soap. In September 1612 it took eight days at 6d a day to pay someone to burn bracken and collect the ashes to produce a year's supply of lye. In June of the same year, 6lb of 'sweete' or scented soap cost 2s 2d and clouded or mottled soap, bought in Halifax, cost 4s. Over a century later, it was calculated that a bachelor earning £238 a year from a small business would spend £12 – five per cent of his income – on his soap, starch and blue, a powder for whitening linen.

At the end of the eighteenth century a Frenchman, Nicolas Le Blanc, discovered a means of mass-producing soda from salt. The availability of this cheap alkali benefited householders and the soap industry alike, and soda remained a cheap alternative to soap until 1853 when the soap tax imposed since 1643 was finally lifted. It was William Hesketh Lever, later Lord Leverhulme, who was responsible for making soap available to all but the poorest. His Sunlight Soap, according to an advertisement of 1890, would enable 'a cheerful old Soul to continue to do laundry work. . . . The cleansing properties of Sunlight Soap save years of arduous toil. Reader, prove Sunlight Soap for yourself, and by giving the best article a trial you will do yourself real service.'

A late nineteenth-century advertisement from Mr Straw's House, Worksop in Nottinghamshire, showing soap as an affordable household commodity.

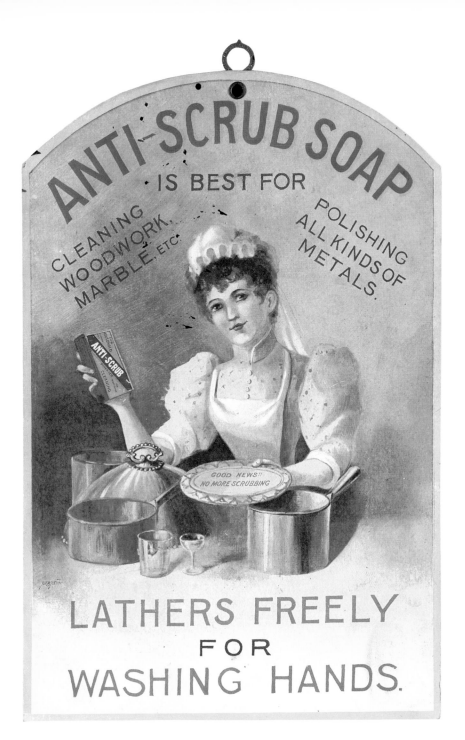

S P O T S and stains on garments too delicate to be washed with the rest of the laundry would be dealt with according to the type of stain. Grease and oil, for instance, were treated with an absorbent powder like ground sheep's hooves, fuller's earth or clay moistened with lye. Lemon and orange juice removed ink and iron stains, and warm cow's milk worked on wine and vinegar stains. Fruit stains were rubbed with butter and washed in hot milk. Drops of candle wax were removed by a hot coal wrapped in linen. Furs were either rubbed with bran and then brushed or treated with fine oils.

All these cleaning remedies were set out in a book published in 1583, called *A profitable boke declaring dyvers approoued remedies, to take out spottes and staines in silkes, velvets, linnen and woollen clothes.* It pays particular attention to the problems of cleaning garments embellished with gold or silk embroidery, as normal washing would make the colours run. The best method to clean a dirty decorated shirt was to place it in urine, leave it in a warm place for half an hour, and then wash it in hot water. Although we might recoil from following this advice, soaking clothes in an alkaline solution like urine was a very effective way to dispel grease and dirt. It was quite usual to place a pan under the privy so that it could be collected for this very purpose. Strong beer or ale could also be used, but the shirt could not be left to dry in hot sunshine.

The first English book that dealt with cleaning remedies for fabrics along with the dressing of leather.

A profitable boke

declaring dyuers approoued re-
medies, to take out spottes and staines, in Silkes,
Veluets, Linnnen and Woollen
clothes.

With diuers colours how to die Vel-
vets and Silkes, Linnen and Woollen, Fustian
and Threade.

Also to dresse Leather, and to co-
lour Felles. How to Gylde, Graue, Sowder, and Ver-
nishe. And to harden and make softe
Yron and Steele.

Very necessarie for all men, speciallye for those
which hath or shall haue any doinges therein : with
a perfite table herevnto, to fynde all
thinges readye, not the like reuealde
in English hereto-
fore.

TAKEN OVT OF DVTCHE,
and englished by *L. M.*

1044. b 99
6

¶Imprinted at London by Thomas
Purfoote, and William Pounsonbie.
1583

L AUNDRY facilities in country houses usually comprised three rooms: a wash-house with its wooden washing troughs and washboards, tubs in which large items could be manipulated with special equipment, and a copper built as a permanent fixture with a fire underneath; a drying loft or closet; and a laundry room for pressing and ironing. The laundry would usually be situated at a distance from the house, often adjoining the stables.

At Erddig in Clwyd, the extensive outbuildings contain a Wet and a Dry Laundry, situated opposite the kitchen and across an enclosed yard. Built in 1770 and maintained with their original features and equipment, they are a fascinating reminder of how the laundry of a wealthy family was managed. The wet laundry has two huge coppers and a vent in the roof to release the enormous amount of steam generated when they were in use. Equipment includes a dolly, a wooden implement resembling a four- or six-legged stool with a handle and crossbar which was twisted backwards and forwards in the tub to force soapy water through the dirty clothes, and a long-handled scoop used for emptying the coppers. There is an upright mangle for wringing out clothes.

The first move towards the mechanisation of washing occurred in 1861 when Thomas Bradford patented a rotary washing machine, the Vowel. It came in five sizes, A, E, I, O and U, and consisted of an octagonal outer case in which a circular drum was rotated by a handle on a wheel. Another section had a series of brass-capped rollers which did the wringing and mangling. A Vowel 'E' can be seen at Erddig.

The Wet Laundry at Erddig, showing the copper, two dippers or scoops, a dolly and, in front, a mangle.

THE Dry Laundry at Erddig has a box mangle, a large table-shaped structure, the upper section of which would have contained a number of weighty stones. As damp sheets or table-cloths were fed through the rollers fitted under the box, the weight of these stones would smooth and press the fabric.

Drying clothes indoors was in fact a last resort, necessary only in wet or cold weather. Racks in the wash-house, the laundry or, in humbler dwellings, the kitchen, would be loaded with washing and hoisted to the ceiling. Domestic manuals advised that these were better used for airing rather than drying clothes, and that a separate drying loft was a preferable option. Such drying lofts were usually built above the wash-house, as shown in a plan of the laundry at Dyrham Park in Gloucestershire drawn up in 1700 by the head gardener, Thomas Hurnall.

However, by the late nineteenth century, indoor drying closets had evolved – brick enclosures built over the water-heating furnaces or hot pipes. Examples can be seen at Erddig and at Berrington Hall in Hereford and Worcester. They hold long movable iron frames which slide out to be loaded with wet clothes. A wire grille over the heating pipes served as a precaution against lost handkerchiefs and socks. Ideally there was dual access to the drying frames: pulled out one way into the wash-house they would be loaded, while on the opposite side they could slide into the laundry where the dried linen could be removed.

The Dry Laundry at Berrington, showing the racks that slide out to be hung with wet clothes, and the elaborate stove for irons.

T Erddig, more careful pressing was achieved using the '4 Box Irons [and] 8 heaters' listed in the 1726 inventory and the 'Seven pairs of flat irons' in another dated 1834. The box iron had a hollow section into which a slug or chunk of metal that had been heated on the fire was inserted. The flat-iron was made of cast iron and was heated directly on the fire or stove by means of a trivet.

The operations of a late nineteenth-century dry laundry are superbly illustrated by the Laundry Room at Castle Ward, Co. Down, where the introduction of special stoves in the 1860s meant the laundress no longer had to heat her flat-irons on a trivet. The stove at Castle Ward is big enough to accommodate a dozen or more flat-irons of varying sizes. A rare photograph of a Victorian laundry was taken at Petworth in Sussex in the 1870s and shows just such a stove in use.

In large households there was a demarcation between the upper laundrymaids who were entrusted with the family's fine linen, and the less-skilled girls who did the household washing and servants' clothes, including the laundry of estate workers, gardeners and stablemen, which could, of course, be very heavily soiled. If the household was not large enough to merit a permanent staff of laundrymaids, the washing would be sent out.

The stove in the Dry Laundry at Castle Ward, with the flat-irons of various sizes ready to be heated.

As households were frequently very large, washing was always carefully recorded before it was dispatched to the laundry, so that when it was returned, it could either be given to the appropriate owner or stored in the right cupboard. This was the housekeeper's responsibility and she might well have kept an aide-memoire to help her with this task. In the seventeenth century at Haddon Hall, Derbyshire, this took the form of a washing tally – an oblong piece of wood, bound with brass and faced with a sheet of transparent horn. The front bore a list of clothes and household linen, and beneath each word was a movable disc that could be turned to show the appropriate number – vital for somebody who could not write. However, it was more usual to record items in a laundry book.

In the very grandest establishments a sorting room was set aside. In *The Gentleman's House*, published in 1864, Robert Kerr recommended that such a room be fitted with bins lined with calico bags for the classification of different articles. These bags could then be lifted into the large wicker baskets, often mounted on castors, used to take dirty clothes to and from the laundry. After washing, they were returned, and the housekeeper would distribute the various articles to their rightful owners, storing the household linen in her own cupboards.

The linen lobby at Lanhydrock, Cornwall, situated next to the maids' bedrooms. There was never a laundry in the house: washing was sent out to the House of Mercy at Bodmin and St Faith's Home for Fallen Women in Lostwithiel – both establishments endowed by the Robartes family.

A L L this organisation sounds wonderfully smooth. There must, however, have been examples of articles lost between the laundry and the housekeeper's room, and no doubt some lost tempers too.

We do know about the management, or rather mismanagement, of the laundry at 5 Cheyne Row in Chelsea, the London home of Thomas and Jane Carlyle. The laundry was the responsibility of the single live-in maid, a source of anxiety to Jane Carlyle during her occupancy of the house from 1834 to 1866. Washing facilities were modest, consisting of a built-in copper – also used for cooking – and an old stone sink supplied by a pump from a well below the kitchen floor. The back garden was 'surrounded with rather dim houses and questionable miscellanea, among other things clothes drying.'

On returning home in November 1864 after a particularly bad attack of illness, Jane was appalled to discover the boiler had burst and the pump gone dry. All her table-napkins were '"worn out" of existence! Not a rag of them to be found and good sheets all in rags.' She then discovered that the maid Mary 'had gone into labour in the small room at the end of the dining room whilst Mr Carlyle was taking tea in the same room. The child was not born till two in the morning when Mr. C. was still reading in the Drawing room.' Carlyle, blissfully unaware of the drama unfolding just a few yards away, had not noticed that the best bed linen had been used during the childbirth and then boiled so violently that it was ruined, or that the missing 'fine napkins' had been used to clothe the baby.

The back garden at 5 Cheyne Walk in Chelsea, where the Carlyle washing was dried amidst 'dim houses and questionable miscellanea'. This nineteenth-century photograph shows Thomas Carlyle rather than the prosaic laundry.

B Y the middle of the eighteenth century there were a number of specialist cleaning shops operating in London. Jane Franklin of Maiden Lane in Covent Garden, for example, placed an advertisement in the *Daily Advertiser* of 1742 offering to clean 'silver and gold laced cloth, buttons and buttonholes.' There were also shops which offered customers the option of having their clothes cleaned by 'Dry Scouring', an early version of dry cleaning. The material would be rubbed on both sides with a mixture of turpentine and fuller's earth, and was then brushed successively with a hard brush, a soft clothes-brush and finally with a clean cloth.

In 1849 a French dyer and cleaner, Jolly-Bellin, accidentally upset an unlit spirit lamp over a table-cloth and was amazed to discover that those parts of the cloth into which the turpentine had soaked were much cleaner than the rest of it. He developed a process whereby soiled garments were first taken apart so that the sections could be cleaned separately, dipped into a turpentine-oil mixture called 'camphene', brushed, dipped again, dried to remove the smell, and then resewn. This process, *nettoyage à sec*, was soon practised all over France and was available in the UK as a postal service, operated by Pullars of Perth from 1866. An improved method, which did not involve the unpicking of garments, was established in 1870 when yet another Frenchman, Achille Serre, set up a dyeing and cleaning business in London.

The 1809 trade card of Thompson's of the Strand in London, advertising their comprehensive mending, dyeing and cleaning services for shawls and fine muslins from India.

THOMPSON,

Dresser & Mender

of

INDIA SHAWLS,

GOLD & SILVER MUSLINS,

VEILS, SILK STOCKINGS, &c.

N:º 135,

STRAND,

nearly opposite the Lyceum,

Dying & Scowering in general.

F. Gullan Sculp.

P. 2. 2816

1809

CLEANING processes were usually carried out on the same premises as dyeing. At the end of the eighteenth century the cost of dyeing a gown varied between 3s 6d and 5s, and a pair of breeches cost 2s 6d to dye. Although this was a relatively inexpensive way of rejuvenating a tired garment, there were inherent problems in the procedure, as Jane Austen discovered in 1808 when she wrote to her sister, 'How is your blue gown? Mine is all to pieces – I think there must have been something wrong in the dye for in places it is divided with a touch – there was 4 shillings thrown away.'

The blue dye that was used on Jane's gown would have been made from either woad, grown in Britain since prehistoric times, or indigo from the West Indies, which also supplied logwood, a brown colouring. Madder, a fast-growing climbing herb, was one of the most versatile dyes – its roots produced a whole range of reds when mixed with minerals or mordants. A more expensive imported red dye was cochineal, made from the crushed bodies of South American insects. Yellows were obtained from the native plants saffron and weld. Dyers could not fix the colour green, so covered blue with yellow, until a Bavarian, Oberkampf, produced a fast green dye from chemicals in 1809.

At Lavenham Guildhall in Suffolk, the National Trust has created a garden containing all the plants used by the Guild of Weavers, Spinners and Dyers to create natural plant dyes. There are nearly thirty different plants, including familiar flowers like asters and golden rod for yellow and the root of flag iris for black. Herbs include sweet woodruff, whose leaves give a green dye, parsley for deep cream, and the root of lady's bedstraw for a striking coral pink.

An early nineteenth-century illustration of haematoxylon campechianum or logwood, a West Indian plant that provided brown colour for dyeing.

D Blair ad siccurl. et lith.   M&N.Hanhart imp

HÆMATOXYLON CAMPECHIANUM, L.

BEFORE the advent of pavements, proper drainage and the collection of rubbish, both town- and country-dwellers waged a constant battle to keep their clothes clean. Wooden overshoes, such as clogs and pattens, lifted the wearer above the street level, but were of limited effect. They must also have been difficult to wear. Elizabeth Pepys experienced problems with hers when out walking with her husband in 1660: 'Called on my wife and took her to Mrs Pierce's, she in the way being exceedingly troubled with a pair of new pattens and I vexed to go so slow, it being late.'

There are frequent references in Pepys's diary to the incredibly dusty conditions of London's streets and open spaces in the summer months. The pollution of city air by the sea coal burned in homes and businesses added to the environmental grime collected on clothing. John Evelyn even wrote a pamphlet, *Fumifugium*, in the hope something could be done about it. It was inevitable that people travelling on rough country roads in inclement weather would finish the day completely covered with mud, and even those who opted to travel by coach found that the vehicles offered little protection against the elements – passengers were frequently forced to disembark after breakdowns. Things were not much different in the early days of motoring. Small wonder that the laundress was so often a vital member of the household.

Detail from Edward Penny's engraving, 1764, of a maid mopping up a London pavement after a rain shower. She is shown wearing pattens which were so necessary to lift the wearer above street level.

I N the sixteenth and seventeenth centuries clothes were either stored flat in chests or coffers, or hung on pegs in presses, large wooden cupboards often built into the recess of a bedroom wall like the one that has survived intact at Townend in the Lake District. The press, dated 1672, was built in the Small Bedroom along with a separate linen closet and a panelled closet. Chests and coffers were generally made of cypress as it was believed that moths were deterred by the particular scent of this wood.

The 1542 inventory of Lord and Lady Lisle's household goods shows how the contents of their wardrobes were disposed. The largest chest in the house – of cypress – contained Lord Lisle's bulky fur-lined gowns, while those belonging to Lady Lisle were kept in a round chest of 'whyte bordes'. Her nightgowns and kirtles were laid flat in a chest made from fir wood, and separate accessories like sleeves, partlets, hoods and frontlets were stored in a 'flat trussing coffer'. A painted coffer contained the head-dress billiments that were not jewelled or made of gold; linen items like neckwear and smocks were stored separately.

From about 1550 chests and travelling coffers were fitted with a small hanging box below the lid. Called a tille, it was partitioned so that it could contain a number of different fashion accessories like jewellery and ribbons.

The King's Closet or Dressing-Room, at Knole, Kent, furnished as it would have been in the seventeenth century. Under the window is an elaborately carved cassone or coffer where clothes were stored.

MOTHS were the greatest enemy of clothes kept in store, and the sixteenth-century book of advice on cleaning fabrics (see p.10) also included recipes to deal with this hazard. A 'very good' method for the summer months was to sprinkle powdered elecampane root and dried orange peel amongst the clothes. Wormwood, or artemesia, was recommended as an effective deterrent against moths and fleas by Thomas Tusser, agricultural writer and poet, in *Five Hundreth Points of Good Husbandrie,* 1559:

> While wormwood hath seed, get a handful or twain
> To save against March to make flea to refrain,
> Where chamber is sweeped and wormwood is strown,
> No flea for his life dare abide to be known.

Additionally, the herb garden would provide the housewife with pungent herbs – cotton lavender, bay leaves, thyme, rosemary and tansy – to place amongst linen and clothing. A bill dated 1564 from Elizabeth I's apothecary, John Hemingwey, shows that he supplied perfume, rose-water and cloves every two or three days to put in the royal presses and chests. Heavy, fur-lined gowns were perfumed with benjamin, storax and sweet-smelling gums; linen was kept sweet by bags of powdered orris root, violet and damask. Those who did not have access to a garden could buy their simples, or herbs, from apothecaries, which in London were grouped together in Bucklersbury, explaining Falstaff's comment in *The Merry Wives of Windsor* that he is not one who will 'smell like Bucklersbury in simple-time.'

The Brewhouse at Moseley Old Hall, Staffordshire, with the spices and herbs used to make
up scent bags to be put in with clothes.

I N the mid-seventeenth century a hybrid form of storage came into vogue. Half cabinet, half chest, it developed into the chest of drawers. Samuel Pepys, always eager to keep up with the latest mode, bought 'a fair chest of drawers' on 1 July 1661.

This storage transition was in fact fashion-led. In the sixteenth and early seventeenth centuries clothes were heavy and bulky and laying them on top of one another would not necessarily cause them any harm. But the lighter, thinner fabrics that came to Britain at the Restoration – the silks and satins shown in the portraits of Peter Lely, Jacob Huysmans and Godfrey Kneller – would have been crushed and damaged if they were compressed in this way. Careful folding and storing of items of dress in separate drawers minimised this risk, and a chest of drawers also conveniently accommodated the wide range of accessories demanded by fashion in the same storage unit.

Chests of drawers were kept in the bedroom. Here too, for the sophisticated, would be a dressing-table, flanked by a pair of candlesticks, and covered with a fringed table-carpet and a toilette of linen. When John Evelyn visited Hampton Court on 9 June 1662, he noted that Charles II's new Queen, Catherine of Braganza, had a 'great looking glass and toilet of beaten and massive gold.' This is an early instance of the use of the word toilet to mean the accessories of dressing rather than the cover on the table. Some very fine toilet sets, or toilettes, were made at this time, and would have included a looking-glass, salvers, caskets, covered bowls and even matching nightgowns, caps and slippers. The toilet set made for Lyonel Tollemache, 4th Earl of Dysart, can be seen at Ham House, Surrey.

A rare depiction of a seventeenth-century bedroom, showing candlesticks flanking a dressing-table, which is covered with a fringed table-carpet and a toilette of linen. The open dressing-box probably has a looking-glass in its lid. One of five engravings by Edmond Marmion, c. 1640 from a collection made by Samuel Pepys.

I N seventeenth- and early eighteenth-century English houses of substance, the chief bedchambers were to be found on the ground floor, in a suite of rooms known as an apartment, situated at the corners of the main block. The suite consisted of bedchamber, ante-room and withdrawing room, in decreasing order of privacy. Even so, the bedroom was surprisingly public, used for ceremonial visits, interviews and even for dealing with staff. As a result, small, more private 'cabinet' rooms — one of which would be a dressing-room — were provided at the end of the sequence.

The development of reception rooms in the eighteenth century meant that the concept of the apartment lost some of its validity, and the bedroom became a private rather than a public room. However, bedroom accommodation continued to be laid out in suites of rooms, including a dressing-room and a powdering closet — a special room for the messy process of applying powder to the fashionable eighteenth-century wigs: an example can be seen off one of the bedrooms at Lyme Park in Cheshire.

As fashions changed, so did the decor, and few eighteenth-century dressing-rooms have survived in their original condition. The Boudoir at Attingham Park in Shropshire, an exquisite example of neo-classical taste, is therefore exceptional, and contemporary descriptions like that of the cabinet-maker Thomas Sheraton provide most of our knowledge of dressing-room furnishings of the period: 'The dressing-room exhibits the toilet table and commode with all the little affairs requisite to dress, as bason-stands, stools, glasses, and boxes with all the innocent trifles of youth.' At this time the dressing-table could be a simple table, a knee-hole type with cupboards or drawers on either side, or a chest of drawers with a top 'dressing' drawer.

The Boudoir at Attingham Park, designed by George Steuart in the 1780s.

B<small>Y</small> the eighteenth century the chest of drawers had become a complex piece of furniture – the snobbish appeal of which is apparent in a reference from Samuel Richardson's novel, *Clarissa*, 1747–8. Her clothes are removed from the 'trunks they came in, into an ample mahogany repository, where they will lie at full length, which has drawers in it for linen. A repository, says he, that used to hold the richest suits which some of the nymphs put on when they are to be dressed out to captivate or to ape quality.'

The pattern books of Thomas Chippendale and his contemporary designers have a large number of designs for clothes-presses with doors in the upper portion, enclosing sliding shelves or trays, and drawers below. An example of this kind of press, the work of Chippendale c.1767, can be seen in the Crimson Bedroom at Nostell Priory in Yorkshire. By the end of the eighteenth century it had become more usual for ladies to hang their clothes from pegs rather than to store them flat. Accordingly, wardrobes became larger and more substantial pieces of furniture, with a central clothes-press section flanked by slightly recessed hanging cupboards.

In his Drawing Book of 1791–4, Thomas Sheraton included a new feature in his wardrobe designs: 'the wings have each of them arms, to hang clothes on, made of beech, with a swivel in their centre, which slips onto an iron rod fixed by plates screwed on to each side of the wings.' Despite the obvious advantages of this system, it was not one that was developed, and coat-hangers were virtually unknown until the 1880s.

Detail of the mid-eighteenth-century clothes-press made by Thomas Chippendale for the Crimson Bedroom at Nostell Priory, showing the sliding shelves lined with marble paper.

E LEGANCE was the guiding principle of Georgian design, whether it be the furniture created for the daily ritual of dressing or the more grandiose furniture in the saloon. Thomas Chippendale published designs for dressing-tables in the 1760s that celebrated the rococo style with carved scrolls, elegant gilt ornament and swags of fringed drapes hanging across the recess under the central drawer.

John Zoffany's portrait of an actress c.1764–5, depicts her performing a scene from a play in her dressing-room. The elegant dressing-table is swathed in festoons of fabric, and a number of jars and pots are scattered over its surface. Cosmetics were used in ever-increasing variety at this time, and could include scent bottles of glass, enamelled copper and gold; ceruse, a mixture of white lead and vinegar to lighten the complexion; jars of jasmine pommade for the hair and bear's grease as the basis for creams and rouges.

Improved glass-making techniques in the last quarter of the eighteenth century led to the production of the cheval-glass. These tall mirrors stood on four-legged frames and could be tilted, giving a full-length view of the user.

Zoffany's painting at Petworth, Sussex, showing the actress Mrs Cibber as the Widow Bellmour from The Way to Keep Him *by Arthur Murphy, 1764. She stands next to her elaborately festooned dressing-table with its cosmetic pots and a book.*

F ASHIONABLE Victorian households could boast entire bedroom suites of furniture, thanks to the growing number of craftsmen that had embraced the latest mechanical processes. Firms like Jackson & Graham of Oxford Street in London produced suites comprising a dressing-table, washstand, wooden towel rail, wardrobe, and a free-standing toilet- or cheval-glass.

From the 1830s, clothes were hung in wardrobes by means of 'coat-hangers' – not wooden hangers, but loops sewn into a garment at the back. The modern coat-hanger did not make its appearance until the 1880s when 'mantle shoulders' were used in shops to display clothes. Even as late as 1900 the author of a book entitled *Clothes and a Man* had to explain the concept to his readers, 'a good tailor will give you a shoulder for every coat that you may buy.' Late Victorian coat-hangers can be seen in the substantial wardrobes in the Footmen's Livery Room at Lanhydrock.

If clothes were put away for any length of time, they needed protection from dust and damp. Each item would be carefully wrapped in paper, placed in a labelled calico bag and hung up in a store-room. However, from the 1860s, when dresses once again became very bulky, this method was no longer practical. Instead, skirts were unpicked at the waistband and draperies and trimmings removed so that they could be laid flat, which would, hopefully, avoid creasing.

The Footmen's Livery Room in the attic at Lanhydrock where coats, waistcoats and breeches were brought to be cleaned and repaired. The late nineteenth-century livery shown here belonged to the Tregoning family of Landue, another Cornish house.

MODERN visitors to Victorian country houses marvel at the extent and sophistication of the service quarters. The actual number of staff employed was smaller than in earlier centuries, but more sophisticated equipment was now available to them. In the sprawling service area at Penrhyn Castle, an extraordinary neo-Norman keep in North Wales, the brushing-room overlooks the kitchen court. Here servants came to brush the clothes of the Douglas Pennant family – coats caked in mud from the hunting field, and long skirts that had trailed through the dust and dirt. It is, in fact, the one room where male and female servants, usually strictly segregated, were able to mix. Depressions in the stone floor indicate where they stood, out of sight of both the housekeeper and the butler.

The valet would look after a gentleman's dress, ensuring that his wardrobe was in good repair. His female counterpart was the lady's maid. At Uppark in Sussex, H.G. Wells's mother, Sarah, acted as lady's maid to Lady Fetherstonhaugh. She had served a four-year apprenticeship with a dressmaker which stood her in good stead, for she was expected not only to dress and undress her mistress, but to wash her lace and fine linen and keep her wardrobe in an immaculate state of repair.

Some households would include a seamstress to organise the minor repair of the family's clothes. At Petworth at the beginning of the twentieth century, the Leconfields brought in a seamstress, Maria Cummings, on certain days each week. For the rest of the time she undertook dressmaking at her home in the town, now a Cottage Museum.

The Rose Dressing-Room at Felbrigg Hall, Norfolk, showing the nineteenth-century washstand.

B Y the end of the nineteenth century increased opportunities for long-distance travelling meant that more complex arrangements were required for the transportation and storage of clothes. Cecil Beaton never forgot the extraordinary array of luggage that his glamorous Aunt Jessie took with her to Paris on her regular shopping expeditions before the First World War:

> [Her] enormous black trunks with gilt hinges and locks ... were filled with dresses, others with shoes and corsets, ribbons and ruffs, and aigrettes done up in black tissue paper, or materials with which to make more dresses; beaded embroidery by the yard, and lengths of velvet, brocade, lamé, and chiffons gaily iridescent with sequins. One particularly large box was entirely filled with face lotions, pots of cream, boxes of powder and beautifiers of every description. Then there were the hat boxes – great square containers that held six hats apiece. In those days, mesh moulds were pinned on the sides, top and bottom of a box so that the crown of a hat could be placed over the mould and fixed into place by a long hatpin piercing the mesh. In such a manner, six hats could travel in a box without being crushed.

Both practicality and the desire for comfort on longer journeys meant that the boned bodices and wide skirts designed for travel in the eighteenth century had long been rejected. Instead fashion built on the plainer, more serviceable styles of the servant classes which could be easily cleaned – belted wool great coats with high velvet-lined collars and layers of capes fixed over the shoulders for warmth were worn throughout the century, and frequently handed down within the family. In the early twentieth century the increasing popularity of motoring made the 'cold-excluding, rain-resisting and dust-proof clothing' designed by Burberry wardrobe essentials. The range included hats with dust-proof veils for women, caps and goggles for men, and a summer-weight coat of silk gaberdine. However, as the latest Teflon-coated fibres appear in the shops today, it is clear that we consider the battle to keep our clothing clean is one that has never yet been satisfactorily won.

A lady's fitted travelling dressing-case, c.1900 from Castle Ward.

Care of Clothes

Shelley Tobin, curator of the National Trust's Costume Collection at Killerton, advises how to look after old and valuable clothes and accessories:

❧ Store clothes in a clean, dry place, away from extremes of temperature. Damp basements and dusty, leaking roof-spaces with water tanks are not a good idea: most textiles before 1910 were made of organic fibres which will swell in moist conditions and shrink in a dry atmosphere, eventually splitting and causing holes to appear.

❧ Metal cupboards and shelves are preferable to wooden ones, which can leach acids and discolour textiles over a long period of time. However, as specially made storage units are expensive, cupboards or acid-free cardboard boxes lined with acid-free tissue paper are cheaper and effective alternatives. If possible, garments and small textiles should be laid flat between layers of acid-free tissue paper; larger items should be stored with as few folds as possible. Pad out any folds with a roll of tissue paper, but do not be tempted to over pad, or make sharp creases in the material as this can lead to splitting.

❧ When packing clothes, always place lighter objects on top of heavier ones, and never try to cram too many into one box: not only is this bad for the garments, squashing and creasing them, and reducing air-circulation, but it can also make a box impossibly heavy and awkward to lift! This is particularly the case with heavily beaded items.

❧ Cover metal buttons, buckles or clasps with acid-free tissue paper to prevent staining, rubbing or catching.

❧ Large textiles like patchwork quilts should be rolled right-side-out around a drain-pipe or PVC tube buffered with tissue paper, making as few sags and creases as possible, then wrapped in a dust-sheet. Washed cotton calico is cheap and widely available, and ideal for the purpose. Use wide white cotton tape to secure the dust-sheet around the roll.

❧ Smaller items such as lengths of lace, trimmings and ribbons may be stored in the same way using a cardboard tube, like the inside of a toilet roll covered with acid-free tissue paper.

❧ Do not attempt to hang up fragile garments which are showing stress at the shoulder or waist seams, or that are heavily beaded or bias cut.

❧ For items that are strong enough to be hung up, use wooden hangers padded with clean polyester wadding and covered with a closely woven cotton fabric such as washed, unbleached cotton calico. Removable – and therefore washable – covers can be made to fit over the hangers. Never use wire or plastic hangers: the thin wire hangers used by dry-cleaners can be pulled out of shape and break, while the brittle plastic ones used in dress shops snap very easily.

❧ Dress collections tend to take up a lot of valuable wardrobe space. Avoid crushing by leaving a gap of about 6–10cm between each garment if at all possible. If items must hang closer together, protect each one with a dust-cover or dress-bag made of calico, as described above – this will help to protect garments from rubbing against and catching on each other, particularly important where dresses with hook fastenings, net, beading and metallic braid trimmings are concerned. The bags should be closed at the hem, and made with a slit at the side, fastening with cotton tapes for easier viewing and access. Never use polythene – it attracts dust, and condensation and mildew can form inside.

❧ Do not be tempted to handle or try on old garments and textiles too often, and when lifting objects, always make sure they are properly supported: for instance, don't pick up a heavily-beaded 1920s dress by the shoulders. If possible, wear cotton gloves when handling your collection.

❧ Do not wash or clean textiles and dresses without expert advice. Old dyes are often not fast, and fibres can react with modern detergents. Woollen fabrics can be cleaned very carefully using a hand-held vacuum cleaner with a nylon mesh screen or a piece of net tied over the nozzle. Never attempt to do this with delicate and ornately trimmed fabrics. If you must remove creases for display, steam rather than iron garments. Remember, heat can damage organic fibres and set dirt and stains into textiles, and the tip of an iron can catch and rip fabrics.

❧ There is no substitute for good housekeeping to prevent pest infestation: although there are many brands of insecticide on the market, these can damage textiles. Regular inspection and scrupulous cleaning of the storage area is the best way to avoid pests like the carpet beetle, which lives on the carcases of dead insects and the proteins in materials like fur and feathers, from infesting your collection.

❧ New acquisitions should be carefully inspected for pests and mould, and treated by gentle brushing or vacuuming if possible. Consult a textile conservator about serious infestations. Isolate vulnerable items made of fur, feathers and wool from the main collection for several months, or for the duration of the insect's life-cycle.

❧ Ideally, no natural light should be admitted into the storage area: black-out curtains or blinds behind curtains can help to minimise light levels. Never leave items in direct sunlight – continued exposure to natural light can cause irreparable damage to textiles, and eventually dyes will fade and fibres split.

Household Management

Margaret Willes examines the tasks of the housekeeper, the nursery maids, the butler and the cook, focusing wherever possible on specific individuals – Mrs Garnett, the eighteenth-century housekeeper at Kedleston, Derbyshire, and Mrs Coad, who presided over the Victorian kitchens at Lanhydrock, Cornwall – to provide a fascinating insight into the lives of the men and women behind the daily organisation of Britain's country houses.

Country House Estates

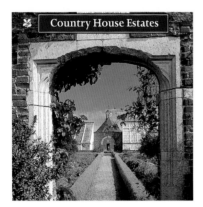

This companion guide to *Household Management* investigates the out-buildings and their personnel – from the land agent and the laundrymaids to the gardener, gamekeeper and the stable lads. Once again Margaret Willes uses the anecdotal evidence of employers and their servants to bring the past to life in an exciting and vivid manner.

Memories of Childhood

What was it like to grow up in a great country house or to serve as an apprentice at the Quarry Bank cotton mill in Cheshire? Drawing on the memoirs of land-owners and servants, rich and poor, Margaret Willes gives an evocative account of childhood over five centuries – how children lived and dressed, their toys and books, and a chronicle of changing attitudes towards their place in the household.